W9-BKH-367

Grasslands
INSIDE OUT

James Bow

CRABTREE
Publishing Company
www.crabtreebooks.com

Author: James Bow
**Publishing plan research
 and series development:** Reagan Miller
Editorial director: Kathy Middleton
Editors: Sarah Eason, Jennifer Sanderson,
 Nancy Dickmann, and Shirley Duke
Proofreader: Wendy Scavuzzo
Project coordinator: Sarah Eason
Design: Paul Myerscough
Photo research: Rachel Blount
**Production coordinator and
 Prepress technician:** Tammy McGarr
Print coordinator: Katherine Berti

Written, developed, and produced by Calcium

Photo Credits:

t=Top, bl=Bottom Left, br=Bottom Right

Dreamstime: Jordi Clave Garsot: p. 16–17; Holly Kuchera: p. 11 (bottom);
Loflo69: p. 13 (br); Vladyslav Morozov: p. 17 (br); Orxystock: p. 4–5;
Pascalou95: p. 12–13; Prillfoto: p. 19 (br); Gordon Tipene: p. 23 (br).
Nature Picture Library: Elio Della Ferrera: p. 21 (br); Troels Jacobsen/
Arcticphoto: p. 22–23. Shutterstock: BGSmith: p. 9 (br); EcoPrint: p. 14–15;
Karel Gallas: p. 3; Kletr: p. 26–27; MilousSK: p. 28 (b); Moizhusein: p.
28–29; Pictureguy: p. 8–9; J Reineke: p. 15 (tr); SNEHIT: p. 10–11; Oleg
Znamenskiy: p. 6–7. Superstock: Minden Pictures: p. 25 (br). Wikimedia
Commons: Justin "Giustino" Clements: p. 1, p. 20–21; Famartin: p. 24–25;
Arthur Rothstein, for the Farm Security Administration: p. 27 (br).

Cover: Shutterstock: Andrej Sevkovskij; Mari Swanepoel (br).

Library and Archives Canada Cataloguing in Publication

Bow, James, 1972-, author
 Grasslands inside out / James Bow.

(Ecosystems inside out)
Includes index.
Issued in print and electronic formats.
ISBN 978-0-7787-0633-5 (bound).--
ISBN 978-0-7787-0706-6 (pbk.).--
ISBN 978-1-4271-7647-9 (pdf).--ISBN 978-1-4271-7641-7 (html)

 1. Grassland ecology--Juvenile literature. 2. Grassland
animals--Juvenile literature. I. Title.

QH541.5.P7B68 2014   j577.4   C2014-903754-6
                                      C2014-903755-4

Library of Congress Cataloging-in-Publication Data

Bow, James.
 Grasslands inside out / James Bow.
  pages cm. -- (Ecosystems inside out)
 Includes index.
 ISBN 978-0-7787-0633-5 (reinforced library binding)
 -- ISBN 978-0-7787-0706-6 (pbk.) --
 ISBN 978-1-4271-7647-9 (electronic pdf) --
 ISBN 978-1-4271-7641-7 (electronic html)
 1. Grassland ecology--Juvenile literature. 2. Grasslands--
Juvenile literature. I. Title.

 QH541.5.P7B68 2015
 577.4--dc23
                                      2014020967

Crabtree Publishing Company
www.crabtreebooks.com   1-800-387-7650

Printed in Hong Kong/082014/BK20140613

Published in Canada
Crabtree Publishing
616 Welland Ave.
St. Catharines, Ontario
L2M 5V6

Published in the United States
Crabtree Publishing
PMB 59051
350 Fifth Avenue, 59th Floor
New York, New York 10118

Published in the United Kingdom
Crabtree Publishing
Maritime House
Basin Road North, Hove
BN41 1WR

Published in Australia
Crabtree Publishing
3 Charles Street
Coburg North
VIC, 3058

Contents

What Is an Ecosystem?

An **ecosystem** is made up of **organisms**, the environment in which they live, and their **interrelationships**. Organisms need many things to survive, including sunlight, water, air, soil, and temperatures that are neither too hot nor too cold. These nonliving things are called **abiotic factors**. Organisms also need each other to live in an ecosystem. Plants turn sunlight into **energy**, while some animals eat the plants and provide energy for meat-eating animals. These living things are called **biotic factors**.

Working Together

In an ecosystem, abiotic and biotic factors work together. The organisms of an ecosystem are **interdependent**. This means that if one part of an ecosystem changes, other parts can be affected, too.

Ecosystems Large and Small

An ecosystem can stretch for thousands of miles (kilometers) or it can be as small as your backyard. A **biome** is a large geographical area containing a number of similar plants, animals, and environments.

Where the Deer and the Antelope Play

Grasslands are areas in which grasses are the main plant life, although small shrubs and trees are often found. Grasslands are usually dry, and get about 24 to 60 inches (610 to 1,524 mm) of rain per year. Grasslands usually have mild temperatures ranging from 23 to 68 degrees Fahrenheit (-5 to 20 °C). However, colder and hotter grassland areas also exist. Grasslands are found on one quarter of Earth's land and on every **continent** except Antarctica.

What Is a System?

A **system** is a group of separate parts that work together for a purpose. The abiotic parts of an ecosystem support the life within it as the organisms interact with all the factors. Sunshine, water, soil, plants, and animals are some of the parts that make up an ecosystem. Each abiotic and biotic part plays an important role within the ecosystem. The ecosystem needs each part to function properly. If just one part of the ecosystem fails, the whole system can fall apart.

Key

- Deserts
- Grasslands
- Oceans
- Rain forests
- Tundras
- Wetlands

This map shows where grasslands and other biomes are found around the world.

Grasslands exist only in places where the temperature is just right. If grassland areas become much colder, they become tundra. If they become much hotter and drier, they become deserts. If they become wetter, they become forests.

5

Energy in Ecosystems

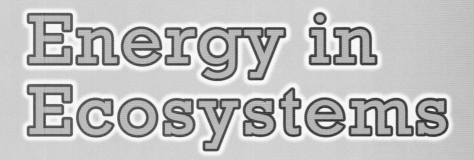

sun

The energy in an ecosystem comes from the sun, and it is spread through the ecosystem as food. Organisms eat other types of organisms to survive. This is called a **food chain**. Most animals eat many different **species**, so a better way to show their relationships is as a **food web** made up of interlinking food chains.

Moving the Energy Up

Every food chain includes three types of organisms. At the bottom of the food chain are the producers. These are plants and other organisms that trap energy from sunlight in their **chlorophyll**, and use it to change water and carbon dioxide into sugar. This process is called **photosynthesis**.

Next in the chain are consumers. These are animals that eat plants for their energy, and animals that eat the plant-eating animals. Animals that eat plants are called herbivores. Those that eat animals are called carnivores. Animals that eat both plants and animals are omnivores.

The last link in the chain are decomposers. These are organisms, such as **bacteria** and **fungi**, which break down dead organisms. This returns **nutrients** to the soil for the plants to use. The food chain then begins again.

Suited to Grassland

Herbivores must eat a lot of grass to get enough energy. It is easier for large animals to live in grasslands than it is for small animals. For their size, large animals need less energy to survive than small animals do.

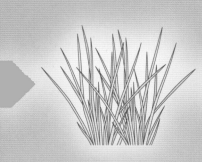

grass

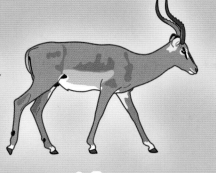

antelope

lioness

This food chain shows the flow of energy from one organism to another.

Eco Up Close

The cow of today **evolved** from grass-eating animals that once lived in Europe, North Africa, and much of Asia. People found that they could tame, or **domesticate**, grass-eating animals. They raised them so they could eat their meat and drink their milk. As people moved around the world, they took domesticated cows with them. This pushed other **native** cattle species, such as the bison and the yak, out of their ecosystems.

Antelopes have long, thin legs that help them run quickly. These animals can run at speeds of up to 60 miles per hour (97 kph). This helps them escape from **predators**.

The Canadian Prairies

The Canadian prairies run east from the mountains of western Alberta, across southern Alberta, and through Saskatchewan and Manitoba. They are a **temperate** grassland, with cold winters and warm summers and a climate that is mostly dry. Trees do not easily grow in most parts of the prairies. However, the climate is ideal for many types of grasses. They provide shelter for birds and insects. They are also food for herbivores such as bison and deer. The herbivores are food for predators, such as wolves and coyotes.

Ideal for Grass

The Canadian prairies have great farming conditions such as sufficient rainfall and a good climate. Wheat grows well there, as does wheatgrass, bluestem, and side-oats. Since the 1880s, people have moved into the Canadian west and pushed out many of the native species. Bison were nearly hunted to **extinction**, as were wolves. All but five percent of Canada's prairie grasslands have been changed to **cropland**. Cropland is land used for farming crops.

People have had to work hard to save the prairie ecosystem. Parks such as Grasslands National Park in Saskatchewan and Wood Buffalo National Park in Alberta keep the Canadian prairie ecosystem as it was before people arrived.

Bison contribute to the ecosystem they live in. Gophers like areas of land that have been grazed by bison. The short grasses help the gophers keep a lookout for predators.

Eco Up Close

Gophers can grow up to 1 foot (30 cm) long. They are found across the Canadian prairies and the northern United States. These animals eat seeds, grasses, grains, and insects. They are food for foxes, coyotes, and wolves. Gophers hide from predators and the hot sun by building tunnels, or burrows, underground.

Farmers believe gophers are pests because they eat crops. Their burrows can also break farm equipment and the legs of animals that accidentally step in their holes. Unlike other animals in the prairies, the gopher **population** has not been harmed by farming. People have tried to control the animals through hunting them and destroying gopher burrows.

gopher

The American Prairies

The Canadian prairies are part of a larger area that stretches across the middle of North America. The American prairies are divided into three zones. In the west, near the Rocky Mountains, is shortgrass prairie. Tallgrass prairie is found in the east, and mixed grass prairie lies between the two. The grasses are shorter closer to the mountains because less rain falls there.

Roaming Free

Large numbers of bison, wolves, and coyotes once roamed the American prairies looking for food. Bison traveled in large herds to find the grasses they needed to eat. Their predators, such as gray wolves, had to travel far to keep up with them. Wolves often hunted in packs, using their numbers to chase down a particular bison until it got tired and they could move in for the kill. When people began to hunt bison, they hunted so many that there was little food left for wolves and coyotes. These animals still live on the prairies, but their numbers are much reduced.

Eco Focus

Along with hunting the bison, people also turned the animals' feeding grounds into cropland. The **range** of the bison and their predators shrank. In some ways, farm cattle have taken over the bison's place in the prairie ecosystem. Who or what has replaced wolves and coyotes? Explain your thinking.

In grasslands, the native grasses have **adapted** to make best use of any rainwater. Unless farmers plant crops that can do the same, they often need to water the crops to help them grow.

Eco Up Close

Bison are **ungulates**. Ungulates are animals, such as cattle or horses, that have hooves. Before people arrived, these beasts lived across the middle and west of North America. Overhunting and **habitat** loss from farming brought the species close to extinction. Without the bison, wolves and bears lost an important source of food. As a result, they began to hunt cattle. People responded by hunting wolves and bears almost to extinction. Today, bison are protected. **Nature preserves** have been set up, and bison are returning to areas where they were once wiped out. Their numbers are slowly increasing.

bison

The Eurasian Steppe

A steppe is a large grass-covered **plain** in North America and Europe. The largest steppe ecosystem in Europe is the Eurasian steppe. It stretches from near the mouth of the Danube River almost to the Pacific Ocean. It includes parts of Ukraine, Russia, Kazakhstan, and Mongolia.

Eurasian steppe

Moving to Find Food

The Eurasian steppe is so dry that only grasses and small plants can survive there. This means that there is less food for herbivores such as horses and cattle to eat. They must move across large areas to find enough food.

Steppe Food Web

The same food web that is found in all grassland ecosystems exists on steppes. The grasses feed and shelter herbivores, such as cattle, while smaller animals such as gerbils hide in the grass or burrow beneath it. Smaller predators, such as foxes, hunt the gerbils. Larger predators eat the larger herbivores. Wolves that hunt in packs survive better on steppes than those hunting alone. The predators stop the herbivore population from growing too large. This would result in **overgrazing** the grasslands. Overgrazing means eating grass faster than it can grow back.

There is little food in grasslands, so the herbivores that live there must travel far to find food. Some people who live in grasslands are nomadic, meaning they move from place to place, following the herbivores they depend on for food and clothing.

Eco Up Close

The horse is a hoofed animal that evolved in North America millions of years ago. The hoof of a horse is an adaptation that allows the animal to run fast to escape from predators and to travel long distances to find food and water. Horses spread from North America to Asia and Africa. **Climate change** in North America wiped out the horses that first lived there. The **descendants** of these horses, such as zebras and Arabian horses, can be found in Africa and Asia today. People who traveled from Europe to North America brought horses with them, and used them to cross the wide prairies.

wild horse

The Veld

A veld is a wide-open plain of mostly grasses or low shrubs. These **subtropical**, dry, hot areas are found mostly in southern Africa. They are especially common in South Africa, Zimbabwe, Botswana, and Namibia.

Rain in the Veld

The African veld has mild winters and very hot summers. It does not often rain on the veld. Rains usually arrive in powerful thunderstorms during the summer. Around 1 to 4 inches (25 to 102 mm) of rain falls in the veld each year. **Droughts** happen every three to four years.

Fires Help Ecosystems

In places as dry as the veld, wildfires happen often. They are usually started by lightning strikes. However, grassland plants have evolved to cope with fire. Grasses recover from fires faster than trees. Grasses regrow from their roots, while trees lose leaves and branches to fire, robbing them of what they need to grow. For this reason, fires help ensure that grasslands stay grasslands and do not become forests. Fires also return nutrients to the soil faster than decomposers, such as bacteria and fungi, can. Some plants can only produce seeds after a fire so, without fire, these plants could not **reproduce**.

About 60 percent of the South African veld has been turned into cropland. Only 2.5 percent of the veld is protected.

14

vulture

Eco Up Close

The vulture is a type of bird that can be found in many parts of the world. Vultures are **scavengers**. Scavengers look for and eat animals that are already dead. Scavenging is a messy business, but it is important to the ecosystem. Vultures have adapted to scavenging by having no feathers on their legs. This means that harmful bacteria do not stick to their legs. As they feed, scavengers break up the dead bodies of animals into small pieces. Without the work of scavengers, such as vultures and hyenas, the bodies would take longer to break down and to return their nutrients to the soil.

The African Savanna

A savanna is a **tropical** grassland where there is enough water for trees to grow, but not enough that the branches of the trees form a **canopy**. As long as the trees do not block the light, sunlight can reach the earth, and grasses continue to grow between trees. The African savanna is the largest savanna in the world. However, there are also savanna ecosystems in many other parts of the world, including Australia, South America, North America, and India. The edges of the American tallgrass prairie are an example of savanna grassland. A savanna is sometimes a **transition zone** between thick forests and drier, more desert-like grasslands.

Living Among the Trees

In savannas, the trees are an extra source of food for herbivores, such as giraffes. Giraffes have evolved long necks to reach the leaves at the tops of trees. Grassland animals have adapted to a habitat that has few trees. With few trees to hide among, **prey** animals, such as wildebeest, have to run fast and in herds to avoid being caught and eaten. Predators, such as lions and cheetahs, have to run quickly to catch their fast-running prey.

Grasslands suit animals that can move far and fast. Lions can run in bursts of speed up to 50 miles per hour (81 kph) to catch their prey, but can keep up that pace only for a short time.

Eco Up Close

The elephant is the largest living land animal. It is found in the savanna and veld of Africa and in parts of India and southeast Asia. Elephants eat leaves, twigs, bark, fruits, and roots. To reach roots, they push over trees and dig up undergrowth. Elephants are a keystone species. A keystone species has a great effect on the ecosystem it lives in. By pushing over trees, elephants stop savannas from turning into forests. Elephants also dig for water, creating waterholes that other animals drink from. Finally, elephants spread seeds by eating plants, and dropping the seeds over a wide area in their waste.

Eco Focus

What might happen if a keystone species, such as the elephant, is removed from the grassland ecosystem?

elephant

The South American Pampas

The Pampas is an area of **fertile** lowlands in Uruguay and eastern Argentina. It covers nearly 290,000 square miles (1,097 sq km). The Pampas is windy and **humid**. Around 24 inches (610 mm) of rain falls throughout the year. Wildfires often break out in the Pampas, which keeps the tree population down. This allows grasses to grow. The regular rains have helped fertile soils to stay wet, rather than becoming dry and blowing away. This has meant the soil has built up. The rich soil makes the Pampas an important farming area.

Most of the Pampas has now been turned into farmland. It is one of the most threatened habitats on Earth.

Holding Down the Soil

As with other grasslands ecosystems, grasses are at the base of the Pampas food chain. Without grasses, herbivores, such as the Pampas deer, would have nothing to eat. The grasses also protect the ecosystem by holding down the soil. Even in times of drought, the roots of the grasses dig into the soil and keep it from blowing away in the wind. If overgrazing took place, the grasses might disappear. If this happened, the ecosystem would become a desert. This is called **desertification**.

18

Eco Focus

Grasslands can occur only in places that are not too dry and not too wet. How could grasslands be affected if areas have too much rainfall?

Eco Up Close

Rheas are birds that can grow up to 5 feet (1.5 m) tall. They live in the Pampas. The birds have long legs, and wings that are so small that they cannot fly. Rheas use their long legs to run from predators, and can reach speeds of 40 miles per hour (64 kph). The birds are similar to ostriches, which are also fast-running birds that cannot fly. Rheas help the ecosystem by spreading in their wastes the seeds of the grasses they eat.

rhea

Montane Grasslands

High up on mountains, temperatures become extremely cold—far too cold for trees to grow. This point is called the tree line. Above this point, but still below icy mountaintops, are montane grasslands.

Grasslands in Miniature

Montane grassland ecosystems are much smaller than grasslands in places such as the Eurasian steppe or the American prairies. However, a web of interdependent species can still be found in montane grasslands. An example of a montane grassland is the Ethiopian Highlands. These are found at heights of up to 5,905 feet (1,800 m) above sea level. Winds from the Indian Ocean blow rain to the Ethiopian Highlands from June to mid-September.

The Ethiopian Highlands are small, like tiny prairies. Small grazing animals, such as the Nubian ibex, eat its grasses, taking the position in the food chain that large bison or elephants have in the savanna. The main predators are much smaller, too. Eagles and Ethiopian wolves eat ibex, and smaller species such as shrews and bushbuck. People have farmed much of the fertile lands of the Ethiopian Highlands. Because of this, a great deal of the natural habitat has been lost. This has made it difficult for the Ethiopian wolf and many other species to survive.

Goats and ibex have adapted to living in montane grasslands. They have strong legs and soft, gripping pads on their hooves to help them climb rocky ledges.

Eco Up Close

The Ethiopian wolf is an **apex predator** of a number of montane grassland ecosystems in Africa. Apex predators are animals at the top of the food chain, which have few, if any, predators of their own. The Ethiopian wolf hunts prey such as mole rats. Unlike other wolves, the Ethiopian wolf hunts alone. It is also smaller than other wolf-like hunters. However, because much of its habitat has been lost to farmland, the wolf's habitat has shrunk. It now lives in just seven mountain ranges. This wolf species is on the brink of extinction.

Ethiopian wolf

Island Grasslands

There are thousands of islands in the oceans of the world. Depending on its location, an island may have the wind, rain, and temperatures needed for grassland. Island grasslands include Ascension Island and the Tristan da Cunha **archipelago** in the southern Atlantic Ocean. An archipelago is a chain of islands. The Amsterdam and Saint Paul Islands in the southern Indian Ocean are island grasslands, as is Clipperton Island in the eastern Pacific Ocean, southwest of Mexico.

With no large predators, Tristan da Cunha is an important stop for migrating birds. Thirteen species of seabirds use the islands as a safe breeding ground.

Little Room to Roam

Like montane grasslands, island grasslands are smaller than most grassland ecosystems. There is less food to go around, and the animals that eat the grasses are usually small species of **mammals**, or **reptiles** such as lizards. Many animals found on grassland islands are visitors from other ecosystems. Some **migrating** birds, that fly to warmer places in the winter, travel to island grasslands. So do ocean animals, such as seals or turtles. Saint Paul Island in the southern Indian Ocean is a **breeding ground** for fur seals, elephant seals, and rockhopper penguins. A breeding ground is a place where a species gathers to reproduce and raise offspring.

Eco Focus

Invasive species are animals or plants that have been introduced into an ecosystem where they did not originally live. Invasive species often have no predators to keep down their populations. How might an invasive species affect a grassland ecosystem? How might the ecosystem change and weaken over time? Explain your thinking.

Eco Up Close

When humans traveled to grassland islands by ships, they brought with them other animals that were not native to the islands. This harmed the ecosystem. Cats and rats from the ships spread across the islands. The cats killed the islands' migrating seabirds, threatening populations of seabirds that had never before had to deal with these predators. People have tried to remove cats and rats from the islands to restore their natural ecosystems.

house cat

Xeric Shrublands

Grasslands do well in places that are too dry for trees to grow but are wet enough for grasses to live. If an area becomes too dry for grasses to survive, it becomes a desert. However, before grassland becomes a true desert, it may become a semi-desert that is similar to grassland. This is called a xeric shrubland. Xeric shrublands exist in very dry places. Xeric ecosystems have many plants that survive on less than 10 inches (254 mm) of rain a year. These include tough bushes and water-storing plants such as cacti. Xeric shrubland is one of the largest land biomes on Earth.

Hot and Dry

An example of a xeric shrubland is an area called the Giles Corridor, in the Great Victoria Desert in Australia. While this may be the largest desert on the continent, in the Giles Corridor, eucalyptus shrubs and triodia grasses grow on the earth. These plants have pointed leaves that grab whatever sunlight they can, while also holding in moisture. These plants provide food for herbivores, such as grasshoppers, crickets, beetles, and termites. These in turn provide food for lizards such as the desert skink. Cold-blooded animals rely on the heat of their environment to warm up their bodies. These animals need deserts because the heat gives their bodies the warmth they need to move around.

Eco Focus

Plants in xeric shrublands have small, narrow leaves to limit water loss. Sometimes when conditions are too dry, they store water in their roots or they greatly reduce their activities, and wait for the rains to come.

Eco Up Close

The southern marsupial mole is a small mammal that lives in the Australian **outback**. It eats insects. The mole hides from the heat of the sun by burying itself underground. It moves around by "swimming" through the loose sand. The mole spends so much time in the dark that it does not need to see. It has adapted to have only partially-formed eyes.

southern marsupial mole

Our Natural Habitat?

People cannot live without grass. Grasses provide humans with most of the food we eat. Wheat, corn, rice, and barley make up half the calories eaten by people, and 70 percent of all crops grown. Grasses also feed farm animals, which provide people with meat, eggs, and milk.

Farming and Grasslands

As people spread across the planet, they took features from natural ecosystems with them. Early humans used cattle and horses to move across steppes and prairies. If people could not live on food provided by the local ecosystem, they farmed the land and grew new grasses.

For a long time, people lived in balance with the ecosystem. Since the past century, however, people have pushed ecosystems too far. They have planted grasses that need more water or nutrients than the ecosystem can provide. They have allowed cattle to eat too much grass, causing the soil to dry up and blow away. This has removed key abiotic factors that keep grassland ecosystems healthy. As a result, in many parts of the world, desertification is now taking place.

Today, wheat is grown on 593 million acres (240 million ha) around the world. That is an area roughly the size of Alaska and Texas combined!

Eco Up Close

In the 1930s, poor farming methods in the American Midwest combined with drought to create the Dust Bowl. Farmers planted crops that could not grow in dry conditions. They allowed their cattle to eat too much grass. As a result, the soil dried out, and the wind blew it away. Huge clouds of soil blackened the sky, turning day to night. Farmers had to change how they farmed. They left **plant stubble** after **harvests** to hold down the soil, and planted crops that could grow well in drier conditions.

Dust Bowl

Protecting Grasslands

Although grasslands are very important to us, the way we use them is putting them under threat. Farm grasses and overgrazing are pushing out native species. People need to use better farming methods. These include leaving plant stubble in the soil after harvest, or returning overfarmed land back to wilderness. This will help protect our valuable grassland ecosystems.

What Can You Do?

Write to your politicians. Demand protection for wilderness areas, and campaign for improved farming methods.

Save energy by eating foods, such as local grains, that do not have to be shipped long distances. Eat less beef so that fewer cattle are kept on grasslands.

Reduce waste. Do not put food scraps into the garbage. Instead, compost them. This will turn them into a form that returns nutrients to the soil.

Campaign for green space in towns and cities. This will return our towns and cities to a more natural state.

Activity:

Make a Xeriscape™!

Your lawn is made of grass,
but is it the right grass
for your ecosystem?
Let's find out!

If the lawn in front of your house needs to be watered regularly to stay green, think about xeriscaping and how using different plants that need less water could make a difference.

Instructions

1. Make a map of your lawn. Show where the paths and plant beds are. Note which areas are wet or in shadow, and which are dry and sunny. If your lawn is too large to map, pick a small portion of it —choose the driest part.
2. Research some of the plants that are native to the ecosystem you live in. Find out what plants in your area grow naturally in drier ecosystems.
3. With an adult's permission, use garden tools such as hoes and rakes to cut away and remove the grass from the dry area you want to replant.
4. Into this area, mix in mulch and seeds, and water them lightly. Measure the water you use so that you use the same amount of water every time.
5. Observe as the lawn grows.

mulch

seeds

The Challenge

Once your lawn has grown, present your results to others. Discuss these questions:

• How well did the seeds you planted grow?

• How much water did they need to grow compared to other plants on the lawn?

• What animals did you observe making use of your plants?

Glossary

Please note: Some bold-faced words are defined in the text

abiotic factors Nonliving parts of an ecosystem, such as water and soil

adapted Changed over long periods of time or many generations to better survive an environment

bacteria Living organisms made up of one cell

biotic factors Living parts of an ecosystem, such as plants and animals

canopy Tree branches with leaves forming the upper layer of a forest. This layer usually blocks sunlight from reaching the forest floor

chlorophyll A green substance in plants that changes sunlight and carbon dioxide into energy, which is stored as sugar and used by the plant for food

climate change A process in which the environment changes to become warmer, colder, drier, or wetter than normal. This can occur naturally, or it can be caused by human activity

continent A landmass, or large area of land, such as North America, Asia, or Australia

cropland Land that has been changed to grow crops

descendants An organism's young, and the offspring of its young

desertification The loss of plant life and soil at the boundaries of a desert caused by drought and overgrazing

domesticate To train an animal to live alongside people

droughts Periods of low rainfall in areas that usually have more

ecosystem A group of living and nonliving things that live and interact in an area

energy The power that nutrients from food provide to the body

evolved Changed over thousands of years to adapt to the surrounding conditions

extinction The dying out of a species

fertile Having or capable of producing an abundance of vegetation or crops

food chain A chain of organisms in which each member uses the member below as food

food web The interlinked food chains in an ecosystem

fungi A kind of organism that absorbs food

habitat The natural environment of an animal or plant

harvests The cutting and collection of crops for food

humid Damp; describing air that contains a large amount of water vapor

interdependent Relying on each other for survival

interrelationships The relationships between many different organisms and their environment

mammals Warm-blooded animals that have lungs, a backbone, and hair or fur, and drink milk from their mother's body

migrating Traveling to another area for food or to reproduce

mulch A mixture that is added to soil to keep it warm and wet

native Originating in a specific location

nature preserves Places where animals and plants are protected

nutrients Substances that allow organisms to thrive and grow

organisms Living things

outback The desert lands in central Australia

photosynthesis The process in which plants use sunlight to change carbon dioxide and water into food and oxygen

plain A large flat area with very few trees

plant stubble The stalks of plants left behind after a crop has been harvested

population The total number of a species in an area

predators Animals that hunt other animals for food

prey An animal that is hunted by another animal for food

range The area that an animal usually travels across

reproduce To produce offspring

reptiles Animals, such as lizards and snakes, that have scales and that rely on the surrounding temperature to warm or cool their bodies

scavengers Animals that feed on the dead remains of other animals

seedlings Baby plants

species A group of animals or plants that are similar and can produce young

subtropical Describing a climate that is cooler on average than tropical areas but that does not have the cold winters of temperate climates

temperate A temperature that is not too hot and not too cold

transition zone A zone between two different types of zones, having some features of each

tropical Describing hot and humid climate

Learning More

Find out more about Earth's precious grassland ecosystems.

Books

Fleisher, Paul. *Grassland Food Webs in Action*. Minneapolis, MN: Lerner, 2013.

Gray, Susan Heinrichs. *Ecology: The Study of Ecosystems*. New York: Scholastic, 2012.

Silverman, Buffy. *Grasslands (Habitat Survival)*. Chicago, IL: Raintree, 2013.

Websites

Ecology Kids is an excellent kid-friendly resource on the environment:
www.ecology.com/ecology-kids

Kids Do Ecology, World Biomes—Grasslands will show you how grasslands work:
http://kids.nceas.ucsb.edu/biomes/grassland.html

National Geographic, Grasslands Biome is an excellent resource full of facts:
http://environment.nationalgeographic.com/environment/habitats/grassland-profile

Visit PBS Journey to Planet Earth for more information about grasslands:
www.pbs.org/journeytoplanetearth/stateoftheplanet/grasslands.html

Visit the website below to learn about some of the careers that you could choose in ecology:
http://kids.nceas.ucsb.edu/ecology/careers.html

Index